INSIDE
SUBMARINES

Thanks to the creative team:
Senior Editor: Alice Peebles
Illustrations: Mat Edwards and Victor Mclindon
Fact Checking: Tom Jackson
Picture Research: Nic Dean
Design: www.collaborate.agency

Hungry Tomato®
A division of Lerner Publishing Group, Inc.
241 First Avenue North
Minneapolis, MN 55401 USA

For reading levels and more information, look up
this title at www.lernerbooks.com.

Main body text set in Avenir Next Condensed Medium 11/15.
Typeface provided by Linotype AG.

Library of Congress Cataloging-in-Publication Data

Names: Oxlade, Chris, author.
Title: Inside submarines / Chris Oxlade.
Description: Minneapolis : Hungry Tomato, [2017] | Series: Inside
military machines | Includes index. | Audience: Grades 4–6. |
Audience: Ages 8–12.
Identifiers: LCCN 2017014446 (print) | LCCN 2017012928
(ebook) | ISBN 9781512450002 (eb pdf) | ISBN 9781512432244
(lb : alk. paper)
Subjects: LCSH: Submarines (Ships)–Juvenile literature.
Classification: LCC VM365 (print) | LCC VM365 .093 2017 (ebook)
| DDC 623.825/709–dc23

LC record available at https://lccn.loc.gov/2017014446

Manufactured in the United States of America
1-41779-23540-4/3/2017

INSIDE
SUBMARINES

American submarine pioneer John Holland in one
of his submarines in 1899

by Chris Oxlade

HUNGRY
TOMATO®

Minneapolis

The torpedo storage room of HMS *Talent*, a modern nuclear-powered attack submarine

Contents

BATTLE MACHINES: SUBMARINES

There is no more powerful weapon in the sea than the submarine. Submarines travel under the surface of the sea as well as on the surface. Speeding along under the waves, these incredible battle machines search for and attack enemy naval ships with their **torpedoes**. They also carry deadly **missiles** for hitting targets on land.

Submarine Characteristics

All submarines need a very strong **hull** to prevent them from being crushed by water pressure when they are submerged. They have tanks that are filled with water for submerging, and emptied again for surfacing. They also have a **propulsion** system that must work without needing an air supply, and **control** surfaces for moving underwater.

Types of Submarine

There are different types of modern military submarine. Submarines are either attack submarines, which attack other ships or ground targets, or they are missile submarines, which carry long-**range** nuclear **ballistic missiles**. Submarines can also be either conventional, with **diesel-electric propulsion,** or nuclear, with **nuclear propulsion**.

First Nuclear Submarine

This is the crew of the world's first nuclear submarine, the **USS** *Nautilus*, which was launched in 1958. The crew is in the control room, concentrating hard as *Nautilus* travels under the polar ice pack.

Modern Nuclear Attack Submarine

This is **HMS** *Ambush*, an *Astute*-class submarine of the British Royal Navy, traveling on the surface. HMS *Ambush* is a state-of-the-art nuclear-powered attack submarine, armed with torpedoes and **cruise missiles**.

Astute-class Submarine

Length: 318 feet (97 meters)

Width: 36 feet (11 m)

Weight: 7,716 tons (7,000 metric tons)

Propulsion: nuclear reactor

Top speed: 35 miles (56 kilometers) per hour

Crew: 98

Dive depth: 984 feet (300 m)

Weapons: Spearfish torpedoes / Tomahawk cruise missiles

THE FIRST SUBMARINES

The first submarine that we know actually existed was built around 1620, but it's likely that shipbuilders had talked about the idea of underwater boats before then. There is a written record of a submarine in 1578. Early submarines used materials and marine technology of the time such as wood, leather, and oars.

Drebbel's Submarine

Naval historians think that the first submarine was built by a Dutch inventor named Cornelis Drebbel in about 1620. Drebbel's craft was like a rowing boat with a lid on top, made of wood and covered with leather to make it waterproof. Oars that stuck out through leather flaps propelled it. This submarine made many trips up and down the Thames River in London, England, diving about 13 feet (4 m) under the surface.

Bushnell's *Turtle*

This strange egg-shaped craft was the first submarine to go into battle. It was built by the American inventor David Bushnell. The craft had just enough space for the operator to sit inside. Around him were controls for diving, surfacing, and steering, and a hand crank to turn the propeller.

hatch

wooden hull

propeller for diving and surfacing

submarine operator

propeller for moving forward and backward

rudder for steering

water ballast

In 1776 *Turtle* was sent to attack a British warship, HMS *Eagle*, during the American Revolution (1775–1783). *Turtle's* operator was supposed to attach an explosive **mine** to the ship's hull, but the mission failed.

Modern reproduction of Drebbel's submarine

Nautilus

Robert Fulton was a famous American inventor. He designed a submarine that he built in France in 1801, called *Nautilus*. It had an iron frame covered with copper sheets and a collapsing mast and sail. Four crew members operated the machine, turning the propeller by hand. Like the earlier *Turtle*, *Nautilus* was supposed to attack ships by creeping up to them and attaching an explosive mine. However, when *Nautilus* tried to sink some British battleships, it couldn't go fast enough to catch up with them.

Turtle

Length: 10 feet (3 m)

Width: 3 feet (0.9 m)

Height: 6 feet (1.8 m)

Crew: 1

Weapons: explosive mines

Top speed: 3 miles (5 km) per hour

HUNLEY AND HOLLAND

Despite the attacks on ships by submarines in the late eighteenth century, it wasn't until the 1860s that a submarine actually sank a ship for the first time. The submarine was the *H. L. Hunley*, which fought for the Confederate side in the American Civil War (1861-1865). It was one of several submarines used in the war.

H. L. Hunley

This submarine was named after Horace Hunley, who paid for it to be built. *H. L. Hunley* was just 39 feet (12 m) long and looked like a metal tube with flattened ends. The crew propelled the submarine with a crank that turned the propeller. *H. L. Hunley* sank three times, killing its crew, including Hunley. The submarine was recovered each time. And in 1864, it sank a Union ship using an explosive charge on the end of a long pole. But the explosion also damaged the submarine, and it sank for a final time.

Holland's Submarine

Submarine designers tried out different forms of power. They found that steam engines could not be used underwater and that the batteries on electric motors ran out quickly. The invention of the internal-combustion engine solved these problems. In 1897 in the United States, John Holland completed a design of his own. *Holland* had electric motors powered by batteries for use underwater, and a gasoline engine for use on the surface. The engine also recharged the batteries. The US Navy bought the submarine, and the British Royal Navy ordered five more. *Holland* is thought of as the first modern-style submarine.

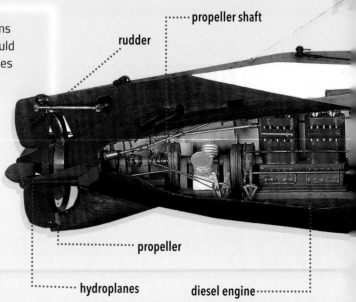

propeller shaft

rudder

propeller

hydroplanes

diesel engine

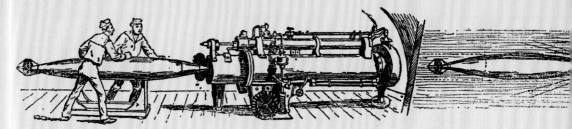

Torpedoes

The torpedo is the submarine's main weapon for attacking ships. A torpedo is like a missile that travels through water. It has a motor to drive it along and an explosive **warhead** that blows up on contact with a ship. The torpedo was invented by British engineer Robert Whitehead. His first successful torpedo, built in 1866, was about 13 feet (4 m) long and traveled at about 7 miles (12 km) per hour. It was originally designed to be fired from surface ships.

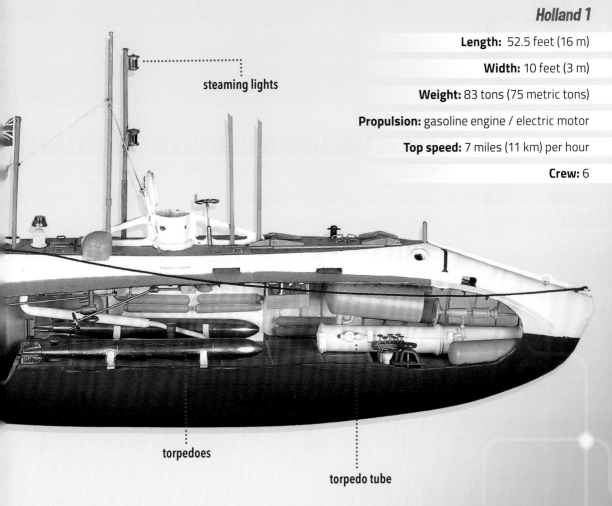

Holland 1

Length: 52.5 feet (16 m)

Width: 10 feet (3 m)

Weight: 83 tons (75 metric tons)

Propulsion: gasoline engine / electric motor

Top speed: 7 miles (11 km) per hour

Crew: 6

steaming lights

torpedoes

torpedo tube

WORLD WAR I SUBMARINES

Most navies had some small submarines when World War I (1914–1918) broke out in 1914. At first nobody really knew how to use submarines in battle, but by the end of the war submarines had had a major impact, sinking thousands of ships. They were used mostly for attacking enemy cargo ships, but they were also used to place mines and attack enemy submarines.

Submarine Forces

Germany and Britain built up large submarine fleets during World War I. At the start of the war, Germany had 29 submarines, or U-boats. Some are seen here in 1914 in Kiel harbor. The British warship HMS *Pathfinder* was the first ship to be sunk by a torpedo fired from a submarine. Of the 351 U-boats built, 178 were sunk, but U-boats sank more than 5,000 Allied ships.

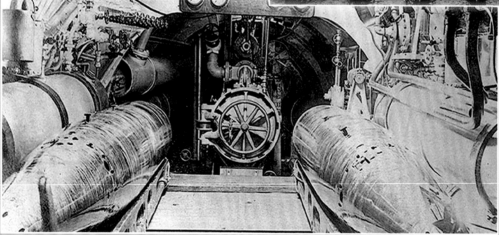

Torpedo Room

This is the torpedo room of an American submarine, showing torpedoes ready to fire. This kind of torpedo was powered by compressed air, which made the propeller spin. At the far end of the room is the inner door of the torpedo tube. This door was opened to load a torpedo, then closed again. The outer tube door was opened, letting in water, and the torpedo was fired. In World War I, torpedo tubes were also used secretly to place mines in shipping lanes and ports.

Engine Room

This picture shows German sailors inside a U-boat's engine room, which was not a great place to be! It was hot and cramped, and it smelled like oil. Nearly all World War I submarines continued to use a combination of **diesel engines** and electric motors. The engines recharged the batteries while the submarine was on the surface. A few submarines had **steam turbines** for high speeds on the surface.

Planes from Submarines

Just after World War I, the British Navy launched seaplanes from submarines. The submarine HMS *M2* had a watertight aircraft hangar, a catapult-powered launching rail, and a crane to pull the aircraft back onboard.

SUBMARINES IN WORLD WAR II

After the success of submarine warfare in World War I, navies continued to improve their submarines. The machines got larger and faster, and they could travel farther without needing to refuel. Weapons also improved, so torpedoes became faster and more accurate. During World War II (1939–1945), submarines played a major part in battles in all the world's oceans.

U-boat Builders

Germany already had 57 U-boats when it declared war in 1939. Soon Germany had more submarines than any other country. Its main U-boat was the Type VII, which was very effective for its small size. The ultimate German U-boat was the Type XXI, which was twice as fast underwater as the Type VII. German U-boats sank more than 2,500 ships during the war.

Inside a Submarine

This image shows the control room of the USS *Cavalla*, an American World War II submarine. Along with controls, the control room has hydrophones (underwater microphones) for listening for the noise from surface ships and **sonar** for detecting other submarines. A sonar system sends out sounds and listens for any that bounce back. If a submarine was being hunted, the crew would turn the engines off and remain very quiet so the hydrophones of enemy ships could not detect it.

Midgets and Minis

Most countries built tiny one-man or two-man submarines called midget subs or mini subs. They were designed to attack ships in enemy ports or in shallow water. Normal submarines could not get into ports, which were protected by strong underwater antisubmarine nets.

THE GERMAN U-BOAT

The German navy had hundreds of U-boats during World War II. Most of these patrolled the North Atlantic, attacking ships carrying supplies between North America and Britain and the Soviet Union.

periscopes used for viewing the surface when the submarine was submerged

command tower

rudder

rear torpedo tube

rear torpedo room

Antiaircraft gun

rear hydroplanes

engine room

ballast tanks

control room

periscopes

Type VII U-boat

Length: 220 feet (67 m)

Width: 20 feet (6 m)

Weight: 848 tons (769 metric tons)

Propulsion: 2 diesel engines, electric motors

Top speed on surface: 20.5 miles (33 km) per hour

Top speed submerged: 9 miles (14 km) per hour

Range: 9,755.5 miles (15,700 km)

Dive depth: 755 feet (230 m)

Weapons: torpedoes, mines, main gun, antiaircraft guns

Crew: 44

Number built: 703

Type VII U-boat

The Type VII U-boat was the most common German U-boat of World War II and the most common submarine of the war. More than seven hundred were built. Its weapons were torpedoes, an 88 mm deck gun and antiaircraft guns.

Making an Attack

A U-boat attack was organized from the ship's control room. With the ship on the surface or at **periscope** depth (just under the surface with the periscopes raised), the crew used the periscopes to figure out the direction, range, and speed of a target. They calculated the direction a torpedo needed to travel to intercept the target, set this direction on a torpedo's guidance system, and fired it from one of the torpedo tubes.

88 mm deck gun used to attack undefended ships

bunks for crew amid the submarine's machinery

forward hydroplanes

U 47

forward torpedo room

forward torpedo tubes

U-boat Tactics

German U-boats stayed on the surface most of the time. They usually attacked at night, still on the surface. They only dived to escape enemy submarine-hunting ships, or for a rare daytime attack. They often hunted in packs to improve their chances of sinking ships. The most successful of all the U-boats was *U-48*, which sank fifty-five ships.

NUCLEAR SUBMARINES

The world of submarines was transformed in the 1950s with the development of the nuclear submarine. In these submarines, a nuclear power plant replaced the diesel-electric system of World War II submarines. This had the massive advantage that the submarines did not have to surface to run their engines. They could stay underwater almost indefinitely.

The First Nuclear Submarine

USS *Nautilus* of the US Navy was the world's first nuclear-powered submarine. It was an attack submarine launched in 1955. This photograph shows the control room of the second nuclear submarine, USS *Seawolf*, with the US President of the time, Dwight D. Eisenhower, trying out the submarine's periscope.

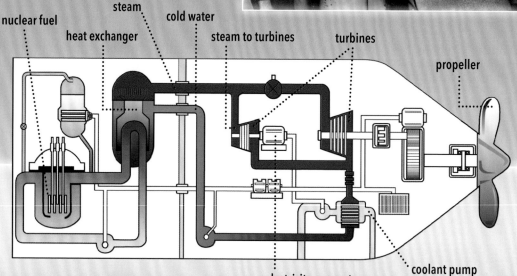

nuclear fuel · heat exchanger · steam · cold water · steam to turbines · turbines · propeller · electricity generator · coolant pump

Submarine Nuclear Power Plant

Most nuclear submarines are powered by a **nuclear reactor** called a pressurized water reactor (PWR). Nuclear reactions in the nuclear fuel give out heat. This heats water around the fuel, which is pumped to a heat exchanger, where it boils water in separate pipes to make steam. The steam is fed to one turbine that turns the propeller and another turbine that drives a generator to make electricity.

Typhoon-Class Submarine

This huge machine is the biggest submarine ever built. It weighed almost 53,000 tons (48,080 metric tons) and carried ballistic missiles. The submarine is a Russian Akula submarine, called a Typhoon-class by navies in Europe and America. The first of these was completed in 1981, and only six were ever built.

Typhoon-Class Submarine

Length: 574 feet (175 m)

Width: 75 feet (23 m)

Weight: 53,000 tons (48,080 metric tons)

Power: 2 nuclear reactors

Top speed surfaced: 25.5 miles (41 km) per hour

Top speed submerged: 31 miles (50 km) per hour

Dive depth: 1,312 feet (400 m)

Crew: 160

Submarines at the North Pole

Because nuclear submarines can stay underwater for long periods of time, they can travel under sea ice. In 1996, USS *Pogy*, a *Sturgeon*-class nuclear submarine, visited the Arctic on a scientific mission to collect samples of water from the Arctic Ocean. It punched its way up through the ice many times during the mission.

19

MODERN SUBMARINES

Modern submarines are extremely high-tech battle machines. They travel secretly through the oceans, hidden under the surface, always ready to complete missions whenever they are needed. Modern submarines have many advanced systems onboard for navigating, communications, tracking other military craft, launching and controlling weapons, and defending themselves against attack.

Attack Submarine

The smooth, rounded hull of a modern submarine is designed for the submarine to move smoothly while submerged, with minimum water resistance. The hull has a superstrong skin called a pressure hull, which resists water pressure when the submarine dives. The fin, or sail, sticks up from the hull. It holds periscopes, communications antennae, and a lookout post. There are torpedo tubes at the **bow** and **stern**, and cruise missiles inside the hull.

Submerging and Surfacing

The submarine has **ballast tanks** on each side of the hull. When the submarine is on the surface, the tanks are empty. To dive, the ballast tanks are filled with water, making the submarine heavier. Once underwater, **hydroplanes** are used to steer the submarine up and down through the water. To surface, air is pumped into the ballast tanks to push the water out.

Crew Jobs

The crew members of a submarine (known as submariners) are highly trained and work as a tightly knit team. Each crew member has a specific job to do. There are members who navigate the submarine, weapons experts, communication experts, engineers who operate the nuclear reactors, and crews who look after the other crews, such as cooks.

Repairs and Maintenance

Modern submarines are hugely complex machines, full of electrical and mechanical systems. These systems sometimes need repairs by onboard engineers and electricians. The systems also require regular maintenance to keep them working smoothly. Every few years, a submarine returns to base for major maintenance jobs such as refueling its nuclear reactor.

LIFE UNDER THE WAVES

Life as a submariner is very different from life as a sailor on a surface ship. For most of their time at sea, modern submarines stay underwater. They can be submerged for months at a time and only come up to resupply. Conditions onboard are cramped, and there is very little contact with the outside world.

Working in Watches

Inside a submarine deep under the ocean, there's no day or night. A submarine keeps working 24 hours a day, and there are no weekends. The crew of a submarine is divided into teams called watches. Each watch works for a certain number of hours before switching to the next watch. Crews regularly practice making an attack or taking action if their submarine is attacked.

Crew Space

Submariners have only a small bunk space to call their own, and a small locker in which to store their belongings. They eat and rest in a small canteen area. Officers have a bit more space, but usually only the captain has a personal cabin.

Keeping Fit

There's no space to run around and stay in shape on a submarine. Submariners lift weights and use exercise bikes. They often have to exercise in whatever open space they can find.

Ready for Emergencies

There's always a chance that a submarine could be damaged in action or suffer a mechanical failure, leaving it unable to return to the surface. If the submarine is less than about 650 feet (198 m) down, the crew can escape using submarine escape immersion equipment (SEIE). They put on a special immersion suit, leave the submarine through a hatch, and float quickly up to the surface. Crews regularly practice for this situation.

WEAPONS AND DEFENSE

The job of a modern submarine is to attack targets at sea and on land, so a submarine has a range of weapons, including homing torpedoes and missiles. Enemy ships, submarines, and aircraft are always searching for submarines. A submarine's main form of defense is to stay deep underwater, but it also has sensing equipment to detect other craft so that it can avoid them.

Ballistic Missile Launch

Some countries operate submarines that carry long-range missiles with nuclear **warheads**, known as intercontinental ballistic missiles (ICBMs). The submarines are part of a country's nuclear deterrent. They stay submerged in secret locations and can launch missiles in case of a nuclear attack, so their presence deters or prevents such an attack.

Rescue Submersible

If a submarine is damaged in an enemy attack or accident and sinks in very deep water, a deep submergence rescue vehicle may come to the rescue. The vehicle is a mini submarine. It dives down to the damaged submarine and tries to dock with it, so that the crew can climb into the mini submarine and be carried to the surface.

Tomahawk Cruise Missile

explosive warhead

infrared guidance system

fuel cell for electricity supply

small wings

Submarine Sensors

A submarine's main sensors are sonars, which figure out the positions of objects in the water. *Sonar* stands for "**so**und **na**vigation **a**nd **r**anging." A sonar system uses sound to detect objects. A passive sonar system detects sounds coming from other ships and submarines. An active sonar system sends out sounds and listens for echoes. The latest submarines have high-resolution cameras and monitors instead of periscopes to view ships on the surface.

electronics control the missile

rudders and elevators to change direction, climb, and descend

turbojet engine

Cruise Missiles

A cruise missile is a cross between a missile and an aircraft. After being fired from a submarine using rocket motors, it flies along, powered by a small jet engine, finding its own way to its target and avoiding hills and buildings. A typical cruise missile, such as this Tomahawk, can hit a target several feet wide after flying more than 932 miles (1,500 km). Attack submarines can launch cruise missiles from their torpedo tubes while submerged.

INSIDE A SUBMARINE

This is a modern *Virginia*-class submarine of the US Navy. It's a nuclear-powered attack submarine that has been in service since 2004. It carries cruise missiles for hitting land targets and torpedoes for attacking ships and other submarines. It can also carry a SEAL mini submarine for special-forces operatives. It has several sonars at the bow, stern, and underneath, as well as a high-resolution light and infrared sensors.

rudder

ducted pump jet pushes the submarine along by creating a water jet from the submarine's rear

propulsion unit in engine room

stern hydroplane

rear ballast tank

nuclear reactor in the reactor compartment

Virginia-class Submarine Stats

Length: 377 feet (115 m)

Width: 33 feet (10 m)

Weight: 8,708 tons (7,900 metric tons)

Propulsion: nuclear reactor

Top speed: 29 miles (46 km) per hour

Range: unlimited

Dive depth: 787 feet (240 m)

Crew: 134

Weapons: torpedoes, cruise missiles

In Command

This is the commander of the USS *Hawaii*, a *Virginia*-class submarine in service since 2004. It's a nuclear-powered attack submarine. A submarine's commander makes the final decisions about its movements and when to send out its weapons. All the submarine's systems are computerized, and information about them is displayed on screens in the control room.

masts for communications antennae and cameras

sail

control room

cruise missiles in vertical launching tubes

torpedo storage

torpedo tubes

forward ballast tank

pressure hull

sonar sphere in the bow dome detects sounds from contacts many miles away

SEAL lockout trunk, an airlock through which divers can enter and exit the submarine

TIMELINE

4th century BCE
Alexander the Great studies the underwater world from a simple diving bell.

1620
Cornelis Drebbel builds the first submarine that we have evidence for and sails it along the Thames River in London.

1863
The submarine *H. L. Hunley* is launched. It is part of the Confederate naval forces during the American Civil War.

1864
H. L. Hunley sinks after attacking and sinking a Union ship. This is the first successful attack by a submarine.

1897
American engineer John Holland launches the first submarine to have battery-powered electric motors for traveling submerged and an internal-combustion engine for use on the surface.

1935
The first German Type VII U-boat is launched.

1801
Robert Fulton's *Nautilus* is launched. It has a sail for surface travel and a hand crank for submerged travel.

1914-1918
Hundreds of submarines take part in World War I.

1939-1945
Submarines play a major role in World War II, sinking thousands of naval and civilian ships on both sides.

1776
David Bushnell builds *Turtle*, a one-man wooden submarine that makes the first submarine attack on another ship.

1915
A German submarine sinks the British ocean liner RMS *Lusitania*, on its way from New York City to England.

1954
USS *Nautilus*, the world's first nuclear-powered submarine, is launched.

1866
British engineer Robert Whitehead invents the torpedo, which goes on to become the main weapon carried by submarines.

US submariners hoist a torpedo during World War I.

1996

USS *Pogy* goes on a scientific mission under the Arctic sea ice.

2004

The first American *Virginia*-class submarine enters service.

1958

USS *Nautilus* becomes the first submarine to reach the North Pole.

FACT FILE

- The most successful of all the German U-boats that operated during World War II was *U-48*. It sank 55 ships. *U-48* survived the war, but its crew sank it so it wouldn't be captured.

- The success of the torpedo that Robert Whitehead designed in the 1860s relied on a mechanism that kept it automatically just under the water surface. The mechanism used water pressure to control the torpedo's hydroplane.

- In 1943, two British mini submarines, called X-submarines, attacked Germany's prized battleship *Turpitz* while it was in harbor. One of the submarines placed explosives on *Turpitz*'s hull, which badly damaged the ship.

- In 1958, USS *Nautilus*, the first nuclear-powered submarine, traveled 1,827 miles (2,940 km) under the Arctic sea ice, visiting the North Pole on the way.

- A modern nuclear sub, such as the British Royal Navy's HMS *Astute*, could stay submerged for 25 years if needed. Its nuclear fuel lasts that long, and it can produce oxygen for the crew from the seawater.

- Russian Typhoon-class submarines were the largest submarines ever built. They were named *Typhoon* by the North Atlantic Treaty Organization (NATO) during the Cold War in the 1980s. They were called Akula-class submarines by the Russians, which means "Shark-class."

GLOSSARY

Ballistic missile

ballast tanks: hollow tanks in the hull of a submarine that are filled with water to make the submarine dive

ballistic missile: a missile that is launched by a rocket, then falls to its target by gravity

bow: the front part of a ship or submarine

control surface: a hinged section on the rear edge of a rudder or hydroplane that is moved to control the movement of a submarine

cruise missile: a missile that flies to its target like a plane, using wings

diesel engine: a type of internal combustion engine that uses diesel oil as its fuel

diesel-electric propulsion: a propulsion system where battery-powered electric motors are used underwater, and diesel engines are used on the surface. The diesel engines also recharge the batteries.

HMS: short for Her Majesty's Ship, a ship of the British Royal Navy

hull: the main body of a ship

hydroplane: a wing-like surface on a submarine that swivels to make the submarine move up or down in the water

mine: an explosive device placed underwater that explodes when a ship hits it

missile: a self-propelled weapon that travels through the air to its target

nuclear propulsion: a propulsion system in which a nuclear reactor creates heat that is used to drive steam turbines that drive propellers

nuclear reactor: a device that produces heat from nuclear reactions in nuclear fuel

periscope: an optical device that allows a submarine's crew to see above the surface of the water when the submarine is submerged

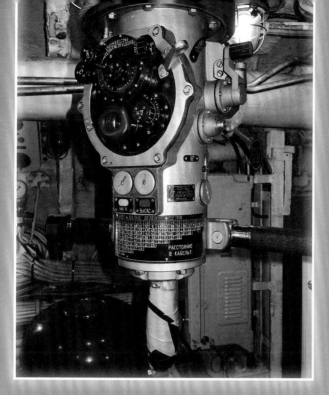

Periscope of a Russian submarine

propulsion: the type of engine that makes a ship move, such as a steam turbine, a diesel engine, or a nuclear reactor

range: the distance that a vessel can travel without refueling, or the distance to a target

sonar: a device that locates objects underwater by sending out sound waves and listening for echoes

steam turbine: a fan-like rotor that spins when steam flows through it

stern: the rear part of a ship or submarine

torpedo: a weapon fired from a ship or submarine that travels through the water to its target

USS: short for United States Ship, a ship of the US Navy

warhead: part of a torpedo or missile that explodes when the missile hits its target

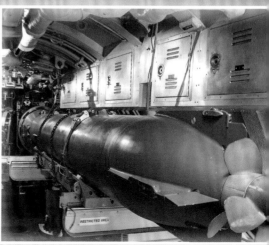

Torpedo room

INDEX

The Author

Chris Oxlade is an experienced author of educational books for children with more than two hundred titles to his name, including many on science and technology. He enjoys camping and adventurous outdoor sports, including rock climbing, hill running, kayaking, and sailing. He lives in England with his wife, children, and dogs.